If you're reading this, thank you for supporting me.

As I've learned to love cooking, I've challenged myself to make the foods I love in the most simple ways. This book is not fancy, nor is it complex, but it's full of easy recipes I think anyone could make and be very proud of. Many people have asked about this book, but I want to give a special thank you to my Husband, Cole, my best friend, Kyllikki, and my dear friend Molly, who has been with me on this every step of the way. Thank you for always encouraging me, and for giving me the strength to carry on. I couldn't have done this without your help, love and kindness.

Contents

Dinner

Jambalaya

Prep: 10   **Difficulty:** Easy

Cook: 35   **Serves:** 4

Jambalaya

1 LB cooked shrimp, chicken and sausage (any amount of each equally about a pound total)

1 tablespoon olive oil

1 onion, chopped

1 bell pepper, chopped

2 cloves garlic, minced

1 can (14.5 oz) diced tomatoes (with juice)

1 cup long-grain rice

2 cups chicken broth

1 tablespoon Cajun seasoning (or to taste)

Salt and pepper to taste

METHOD

Step 1: In a large skillet, heat olive oil over medium heat. Add chopped onion and bell pepper, cooking until softened (about 5 minutes). Add minced garlic and cook for another minute.

Step 2: Stir in the rice and Cajun seasoning, cooking for 1-2 minutes until the rice is slightly toasted.

Step 3: Add the diced tomatoes (with juice) and chicken broth. Stir well, then bring to a boil.

Step 4: Reduce heat to low, cover, and simmer for about 15-20 minutes, or until the rice is cooked and liquid is absorbed.

Step 5: If using cooked shrimp/chicken/sausage), stir it in during the last 2-3 minutes just to heat through.

Step 6: Season with salt and pepper to taste. Garnish with green onions or parsley if desired. Enjoy!

Shepherd's Pie

Prep: 15   **Difficulty:** Easy

Cook: 45   **Serves:** 6-8

Shepherd's Pie

INGREDIENTS

1 lb ground beef

1 onion, chopped

2 cloves garlic, minced

1 cup peas

1 cup carrots, diced

2 tablespoon butter

4 large potatoes, peeled and cubed

1/2 cup milk

Salt and white pepper to taste

1 tablespoon tomato paste

2 tablespoon Worcestershire sauce

1 tablespoon soy sauce

1 cup beef broth

METHOD

Step 1: Boil potatoes in salted water until tender (about 10-12 minutes). Drain and mash with butter, milk, salt, and white pepper. Set aside.

Step 2: In a large skillet, cook the ground beef or lamb over medium heat until browned. Add the chopped onion and garlic, and sauté until softened (about 3-4 minutes).

Step 3: Stir in the tomato paste, Worcestershire sauce, soy sauce, and beef broth. Mix everything well. Add the diced carrots and peas, then let the mixture simmer for about 10 minutes, or until the veggies are tender. If you want the filling thicker, sprinkle in the flour and stir until combined. Cook for an additional minute to thicken.

Step 4: Preheat the oven to 375°F. Spread the meat and vegetable mixture into a baking dish, smoothing it out evenly.

Shepherd's Pie

METHOD

Step 5: Top with the mashed potatoes, spreading them out to completely cover the filling. You can use a fork to create a pattern on top for a little extra texture.

Step 6: Place the assembled shepherd's pie in the oven and bake for 20 minutes, or until the top is golden brown. Let it cool for a few minutes before serving. Enjoy the savory, rich flavors with a perfect balance of buttery mashed potatoes and hearty filling!

Sandwiches, Wraps and Rolls

Buffalo Chicken Wrap

Prep: 15

Difficulty: Easy

Serves: 4

Buffalo Chicken Wrap

INGREDIENTS

1 lb cooked chicken breast (shredded or sliced; use rotisserie chicken or cook it quickly on the stovetop)

1/4 cup buffalo sauce

4 large whole wheat or spinach wraps/tortillas

1 cup lettuce

1/2 cup shredded carrots

1/2 cucumber

Ranch dressing

METHOD

Step 1: If using rotisserie chicken, shred it with a fork. If cooking your own, cook and shred the chicken breast. In a medium bowl, toss the chicken with the buffalo sauce until evenly coated.

Step 2: Slice the cucumber thinly and shred the carrots. Set them aside.

Step 3: Lay out the tortillas on a flat surface. In the center of each wrap, layer the shredded lettuce, shredded carrots, and sliced cucumber. Spoon the buffalo chicken mixture on top of the veggies.

Step 4: Drizzle a little ranch dressing over the buffalo chicken (optional) for a creamy balance to the heat of the buffalo sauce.

Step 5: Fold in the sides of the tortilla and roll it up tightly into a wrap.

Step 6: In a hot pan crisp up the sides of your wrap for a nice added crunch, it also helps keep the wrap together.

Appetizers

Spinach Artichoke Dip

Prep: 10

Cook: 30

Serves: 4-6

Spinach Artichoke Dip

1 block cream cheese

1-1/2 cups mayonnaise

2 cups sour cream

2 tablespoons garlic powder

2 tablespoons onion powder

1 tablespoon salt

1 tablespoon paprika

1 tablespoon chili powder

1 tablespoon black pepper

1 - 12oz package thawed chopped spinach

1 - 14.5oz jar artichoke hearts

2 cups shredded mozzarella

1 cup shredded parmesan

METHOD

Step 1: Preheat your oven to 375°F

Step 2: Drain the artichoke hearts and chop them into small pieces. Squeeze any excess moisture from the thawed spinach (you can use a clean towel or paper towels to press out the liquid).

Step 3: In a large mixing bowl, combine the sour cream, mayonnaise, and softened cream cheese. Stir until smooth and well combined.

Step 4: Add the black pepper, chili powder, paprika, salt, onion powder, and garlic powder. Stir until the seasonings are evenly incorporated.

Step 5: Stir in the parmesan cheese and shredded mozzarella cheese. Keep about 1/2 cup of the mozzarella aside to sprinkle on top before baking.

Spinach Artichoke Dip

METHOD

Step 6: Gently fold in the chopped artichoke hearts and well-drained spinach into the mixture.

Step 7: Transfer the dip mixture to a baking dish (a 9x9-inch or similar-sized dish works well). Sprinkle the remaining mozzarella cheese on top. Bake in the preheated oven for 25-30 minutes, or until the top is golden brown and bubbly.

TIPS & HINTS

- Alternatively, you can throw all ingredients into a crockpot on low, stirring ever 15-20 minutes so it doesn't burn.

Soups

Chicken Tikka Masala Soup

Prep: 15	**Difficulty:** Moderate
Cook: 30	**Serves:** 6-8

Chicken Tikka Masala Soup

INGREDIENTS

2 tablespoon Oil

1 Large Onion (finely chopped)

3 Cloves of Garlic (minced)

1 tablespoon Grated Ginger

1 Large Carrot (diced)

1 Red or Green Bell Pepper (diced)

2 tablespoon Tomato Paste

1 Can (14.5oz) Diced Tomatoes

1 Can (14oz) Coconut Milk

4 Cups Chicken Broth

1 tablespoon Each: Ground Corriander, Ground Cumin, Ground Tumeric, Paprika, Garam Masala, Ground Cinnamon, Ground Cloves, Ground Cardamom

1/2 tablespoon Ground Cayenne (Adjust for personal spice preference)

1 LB Boneless/Skinless chicken (breasts or thighs)

METHOD

Step 1: In a small bowl, combine all the spices and mix well.

Step 2: In a bowl, toss the diced chicken with 1 TBSP of spice blend.

Step 3: Heat 1 TBSP of vegetable oil in a large pot over medium heat. Add the chicken and cook until browned and cooked through, about 5-7 minutes. Remove from the pot and set aside.

Step 4: In the same pot, add 2 TBSP of oil. Heat over medium heat. Add the chopped onion and cook until softened and translucent, about 5 minutes

Step 5: Stir in the minced garlic and ginger, cooking for another minute until fragrant. Add the diced carrot and bell pepper, and cook for another 5 minutes.

Chicken Tikka Masala Soup

METHOD

Step 6: Stir in the tomato paste and cook for 2 minutes, then add the diced tomatoes (with their juice).

Step 7: Pour in the coconut milk and chicken broth. Stir well to combine. Add the remaining spice blend. Stir and bring the mixture to a boil.

Step 8: Reduce the heat and let the soup simmer for 15-20 minutes, until the vegetables are tender and the flavors have melded together.

Step 9: Return the cooked chicken to the pot and heat through for another 5 minutes. Adjust the seasoning with salt and pepper to taste if desired.

TIPS & HINTS

- To enhance, serve with cooked rice or naan bread on the side.

Easy Egg Flower Soup

Prep: 5

Cook: 10

Difficulty: Moderate

Serves: 4

Easy Egg Flower Soup

INGREDIENTS

4 cups chicken or vegetable broth

1 cup corn kernels (fresh or frozen)

2 large eggs

1 tablespoon soy sauce (adjust to taste)

1 teaspoon cornstarch mixed with 2 tablespoons water (optional for thickening)

1/2 teaspoon white pepper (or to taste)

Salt to taste

Choppcd green onions for garnish

METHOD

Step 1: Stir in the corn and simmer for about 5 minutes.

Step 2: If you prefer a slightly thicker soup, stir in the cornstarch mixture and cook for an additional 1-2 minutes until slightly thickened.

Step 3: In a small bowl, beat the eggs until well mixed. Reduce the heat to low. Slowly drizzle the beaten eggs into the simmering soup while stirring gently in a circular motion. This creates the "flower" effect.

Step 4: Add soy sauce, white pepper, and salt to taste. Stir gently to combine.

Step 5: Ladle the soup into bowls and garnish with chopped green onions :)

Lasagna Soup

Prep: 10

Cook: 25

Difficulty: Easy

Serves: 4-6

Lasagna Soup

INGREDIENTS

1 lb ground beef (or ground turkey for a leaner version)

2 cups beef broth

1 (14.5 oz) can diced tomatoes

1/2 cup heavy cream

1 teaspoon Italian seasoning

1/2 cup shredded mozzarella cheese

1 cup ricotta cheese

2-3 uncooked lasagna noodles, broken into smaller pieces (about 2-3 cups of broken pieces)

Salt and pepper, to taste

METHOD

Step 1: In a large pot, heat a little oil over medium heat. Add the ground beef and cook, breaking it up with a spoon, until browned and cooked through (about 5-7 minutes). Drain any excess fat if needed.

Step 2: Add the Italian seasoning, and a pinch of salt and pepper. Stir for another 30 seconds until fragrant.

Step 3: Pour in the beef broth and diced tomatoes (with juices). Bring to a simmer over medium heat.

Step 4: Add the broken-up lasagna noodles to the soup. Stir well and let it simmer uncovered for about 10-12 minutes, or until the noodles are tender.

Step 5: Once the noodles are cooked, stir in the heavy cream (if using) and the ricotta cheese. Let the cheese melt and blend into the soup, making it creamy. Then stir in the shredded mozzarella cheese and cook for another 2-3 minutes until the cheese is fully melted.

Lasagna Soup

METHOD

Step 6: Taste the soup and adjust seasoning if needed (more salt, pepper, or Italian seasoning).Ladle the soup into bowls and sprinkle with additional shredded mozzarella cheese.

French Onion Soup

Prep: 15

Cook: 30

Serves: 4

French Onion Soup

2 large onions, thinly sliced

2 tablespoons butter

1 tablespoon olive oil

4 cups beef broth

1 cup water

1/2 cup dry white wine

1 tablespoon balsamic vinegar

1 teaspoon dried thyme

1 bay leaf

Salt and pepper, to taste

4 slices French baguette or crusty bread

1 1/2 cups shredded Gruyère cheese

METHOD

Step 1: In a large pot or Dutch oven, heat the butter and olive oil over medium heat. Add the sliced onions and sauté, stirring occasionally, for about 10-12 minutes. The onions should become soft and golden brown. This caramelization gives the soup its rich flavor.

Step 2: Stir in the dried thyme, and salt and pepper to taste. If you'd like a slightly sweet depth, add balsamic vinegar and cook for 1 minute.

Step 3: Pour in the beef broth, water, and white wine (if using). Stir to combine.

Step 4: Add the bay leaf and bring the soup to a simmer. Let it cook for about 10-15 minutes to allow the flavors to meld together. Taste and adjust seasoning as needed.

Step 5: While the soup simmers, toast the baguette slices under the broiler for 2-3 minutes, or until golden brown and crispy on both sides.

French Onion Soup

METHOD

Step 6: Ladle the hot soup into bowls. Place a slice or two of toasted bread on top of the soup.

Step 7: Sprinkle with the shredded Gruyère Place the bowls under the broiler for 2-3 minutes, or until the cheese is melted, bubbly, and slightly browned.

TIPS & HINTS

- For a richer flavor: You can add a splash of brandy or cognac when cooking the onions for an even more decadent version.

Sides

Stuffed Mushrooms

Stuffed portabellos with
mozzarella cheese

Prep: 15

Cook: 40

Difficulty: Moderate

Makes: 8

Serves: 4-6

Stuffed Mushrooms

INGREDIENTS

8 large portobello mushrooms, stems removed and cleaned

1 pound Italian sausage (bulk, not in casings)

2 tablespoons olive oil

2 celery stalks, finely diced

2 carrots, finely diced

3 cloves garlic, minced

1/2 cup onion, finely diced

1/2 cup breadcrumbs (optional)

1/4 cup grated Parmesan cheese

1 cup shredded mozzarella cheese

Salt and pepper

METHOD

Step 1: Preheat your oven to 375°F

Step 2: Arrange the portobello mushrooms on a baking sheet, gill side up. Lightly brush or drizzle the mushrooms with olive oil and season with a bit of salt and pepper.

Step 3: In a large skillet over medium heat, cook the Italian sausage, breaking it up with a spoon until it's browned and fully cooked. Transfer the sausage to a plate and drain any excess fat from the skillet.

Step 4: In the same skillet, add 2 tablespoons of olive oil. Sauté the diced celery, carrots, onion, and garlic until they are tender, about 5-7 minutes. Season with a pinch of salt, pepper, and Italian herbs if using.

Step 5: In a large bowl, mix the cooked sausage with the sautéed vegetables. Stir in the breadcrumbs (if using) and Parmesan cheese. Adjust seasoning with more salt and pepper if needed.

Step 6: Spoon the sausage and vegetable mixture into each portobello mushroom cap, pressing it down gently to pack the filling.

Stuffed Mushrooms

METHOD

Step 7: Bake the stuffed mushrooms in the preheated oven for about 15-20 minutes, until the mushrooms are tender.

Step 8: Remove the mushrooms from the oven and sprinkle shredded mozzarella cheese over each stuffed mushroom. Return to the oven and bake for an additional 5 minutes, or until the mozzarella is melted and bubbly.

Step 9: Enjoy! They're great as a main course or as a side dish.

Sweet and Savory Brussel Sprouts

Prep: 5-10

Difficulty: Easy

Cook: 20

Serves: 4

Sweet and Savory Brussel Sprouts

INGREDIENTS

2-3 cups Brussel Sprouts (Quartered)

2 tablespoons Oil

2 tablspoonsButter

1 teaspoon Cornstarch

1/3 Cup Dried Cranberries

1/2 White Onion Finely Diced

3-4 OZ Balsamic Vinegar

1/3 Cup Feta (optional)

METHOD

Step 1: Heat oil in a saucepan or skillet on medium/high heat, once heated add brussel sprouts and diced onion.

Step 2: Cook brussel sprouts and onion until all softened, add balsamic vinegar, cook about 8-10 minutes stirring every few minutes to avoid burning.

Step 3: Once the onions and brussel sprouts start to brown, add in the butter, when melted incorporate cornstarch and stir until everything is fully coated.

Step 4: Cook on high for 5 minutes, allowing everything to crisp up, add the cranberries and remove from the heat, stir all together. Add feta before serving if desired.

Pizza

BBQ Chicken Flatbread

Prep: 10		**Difficulty:** Moderate	
Cook: 10		**Serves:** 4	

BBQ Chicken Flatbread

INGREDIENTS

2 flatbreads (store-bought or homemade)

1 cup cooked chicken breast, shredded or sliced

1/2 cup BBQ sauce

1 cup shredded mozzarella cheese

1/2 red onion, thinly sliced

1/2 cup corn kernels

1/4 cup fresh cilantro

METHOD

Step 1: Preheat your oven to 400°F

Step 2: If you haven't already, shred or slice the cooked chicken. In a bowl, toss the chicken with 1/4 cup BBQ sauce until well coated.

Step 3: Place the flatbreads on a baking sheet. If you like a crispier crust, you can lightly brush the edges of the flatbreads with a bit of olive oil.

Step 4: Spread the remaining BBQ sauce (about 1/4 cup) evenly over the surface of each flatbread.

Step 5: Top each flatbread with the BBQ-coated chicken, spreading it evenly.

Step 6: Sprinkle the shredded mozzarella cheese over the chicken.

Step 7: Add sliced red onions and corn kernels (if using) on top for extra flavor and texture.

Step 8: Place the pizzas in the oven and bake for 10-12 minutes, or until the cheese is melted, bubbly, and slightly golden, and the edges of the flatbread are crispy.

Step 9: Once baked, remove from the oven and sprinkle with chopped cilantro for a fresh, zesty touch. Slice and serve immediately!

Chicken

Chicken Tostadas

Prep: 15

Cook: 5

Difficulty: Easy

Makes: 8

Serves: 4

Chicken Tostadas

INGREDIENTS

8 - 6" Tortillas

1-2 can(s) refried beans (or black beans, if you prefer)

4 cups cooked chicken

2 cups shredded lettuce

1 cup diced tomatoes

1 cup sliced black olives

1 cup shredded cheddar cheese

1/2 cup sour cream

1 avocado

Lime wedges

Oil (any)

Any salsa

METHOD

Step 1: Heat the refried beans in a small saucepan over medium heat, stirring occasionally, until warmed through (about 3-4 minutes). If using black beans, drain and heat them in a pan with a pinch of chili powder or taco seasoning for added flavor.

Step 2: To crisp up the tortillas, place them in a preheated oven at 400-425°F brushed with oil on both sides for about 6-8 minutes flipping to ensure they're crispy and hot!

Step 3: While the beans are heating, chop the lettuce, dice the tomatoes, slice the olives, and shred the cheese.

Step 4: Spread a layer of refried beans over each tostada shell. Add a layer of the cooked chicken, beef, or tofu on top of the beans. Sprinkle shredded cheese over the top and let it melt slightly if you like.

Step 5: Add shredded lettuce, diced tomatoes, sliced olives, and avocado if using.

Chicken Tostadas

METHOD

Step 6: Dollop a spoonful of sour cream on each tostada. Drizzle with salsa and squeeze a little lime juice over the top.

Step 7: Enjoy your tostadas right away while they're crispy and fresh!

Roasted Chicken and Roots

An easy roast chicken with root vegetables like parsnips, carrots and potatoes.

Prep: 15

Cook: 1.5 Hours

Difficulty: Moderate

Serves: 4-6

Roasted Chicken and Roots

INGREDIENTS

Chicken
1 whole chicken (about 4-5 pounds)

2-3 tablespoons olive oil

4 garlic cloves, minced

1 tablespoon dried thyme

1 tablespoon dried rosemary

1 teaspoon paprika

Salt and black pepper to taste

METHOD

Chicken
Step 1: Preheat your oven to 425°F

Step 2: Pat the chicken dry with paper towels. Rub the chicken all over with olive oil. Season the inside of the chicken cavity with salt and pepper. Stuff it with the lemon halves and a few sprigs of thyme or rosemary if you have them. In a small bowl, mix the minced garlic, dried thyme, dried rosemary, paprika, salt, and pepper. Rub this mixture all over the outside of the chicken.

Step 3: In a large bowl, toss the carrots, parsnips, and potatoes with olive oil, salt, pepper, and thyme. Spread the vegetables in an even layer around the roasting pan or on a separate baking sheet if needed.

Step 4: Place the chicken in the pan breast side up. Arrange the vegetables around the chicken in the pan. Roast in the preheated oven for about 1 hour 30 minutes, or until the internal temperature of the chicken reaches 165°F and the juices run clear. The vegetables should be tender and caramelized.

Step 5: Once the chicken is done, remove it from the oven and let it rest for 10-15 minutes before carving. This helps the juices redistribute and makes for a juicier chicken.

Roasted Chicken and Roots

METHOD

Step 6: Carve the chicken and serve with the roasted vegetables on the side. Enjoy!

Chicken Pot Pie

Prep: 20   **Difficulty:** Easy

Cook: 30   **Serves:** 4-6

Chicken Pot Pie

INGREDIENTS

2 Cups Cooked Chicken

1 can (10.5 oz) Cream of Chicken Soup

1 Diced/Sliced Large Carrot

1/2 Cup Corn

1/2 Cup Peas

1/2 Cup Milk (any preference)

1/2 teaspoon Thyme

1/2 teaspoon paprika

1/2 teaspoon Chili Powder

2 Pie Crusts (Store bought or Homemade -See Pie Crust Recipe-)

Salt and Pepper to Taste

METHOD

Step 1: Preheat your oven to 425°F

Step 2: In a large bowl, combine the cooked chicken, cream of chicken soup, vegetables, milk, dried thyme, salt, and pepper. Stir until well mixed

Step 3: Place one pie crust in the bottom of a 9-inch pie dish. Press it into the dish and trim any excess crust hanging over the edges.

Step 4: Pour the chicken mixture into the pie crust, spreading it out evenly.

Step 5: Place the second pie crust over the filling. Trim any excess crust, and crimp the edges together to seal. Cut a few small slits in the top crust to allow steam to escape.

Step 6: Bake in the preheated oven for 30-35 minutes, or until the crust is golden brown and the filling is bubbly.

Step 7: Let the pot pie cool for a few minutes before serving. This allows the filling to set a bit.

Crunchy Onion Chicken Lollipops

Prep: 15

Cook: 30

Difficulty: Moderate

Serves: 4

Crunchy Onion Chicken Lollipops

INGREDIENTS

8-10 Chicken Drumsticks

2 Cups Crunchy Fried Onions

1-2 Cups Italian Dressing of Choice

1 Cup Flour

1 Tablespoon Paprika

1 Tablespoon Pepper

1 Tablespoon Chili Powder

1 Tablespoon Salt

1 Egg

METHOD

Step 1: Preheat oven or air fryer to 380 F. In three bows separate the flour, dressing and crunchy onions. To the flour add all seasonings/spices. Add the egg to the dressing and whisk until fully incorporated. Make sure crunchy onions are in small pieces for breading.

Step 2: Pat dry chicken, cut around the bone closest to the joint of each drum stick, allowing the meat to be pushed down to create the "lollipop" look.

Step 3: Roll each piece of chicken in the flour making sure it is fully coated. After, fully saturate the chicken in the dressing mixture, coat with the crunchy onions, set aside. Repeat until all are coated.

Step 4: Space chicken evenly on air fryer basket or baking sheet, cook for around 30-35 minutes ensuring chicken has reached an internal temperature.

TIPS & HINTS

- Wrap the end of the chicken bone in foil if desired to have a clean end for eating/handling.

Simple Stir Fry

Prep: 10

Cook: 15

Difficulty: Moderate

Serves: 4

Simple Stir Fry

INGREDIENTS

1-2 chicken breasts

1/2 yellow bell pepper (sliced or diced)

1 head broccoli, cut into florets

1/2 carrot, sliced or julienned (to your preference)

1/4 cup peanut sauce (store bought or see recipe for peanut sauce)

1/4 cup soy sauce

1/2 tablespoon cornstarch mixed with 1/2 Cup warm water

2 tablespoon fish sauce

1 teaspoon chili paste (adjust for spice level)

Olive oil (for cooking)

METHOD

Step 1: Slice the chicken breasts into thin strips.

Step 2: In a large skillet or wok, heat a drizzle of olive oil over medium-high heat.

Step 3: Add the sliced chicken to the pan and cook for about 5-7 minutes, stirring frequently, until the chicken is cooked through and no longer pink. Remove from the pan and set aside.

Step 4: In the same pan, add a little more olive oil if needed. Add the broccoli, carrots, and yellow bell pepper. Stir-fry for about 4-5 minutes until they start to soften but are still crisp.

Step 5: In a bowl, mix the peanut sauce, soy sauce, fish sauce, and chili paste. Pour this mixture over the vegetables in the pan.

Step 6: Stir in the cornstarch mixture and continue to cook for another 2-3 minutes, stirring until the sauce thickens and everything is well coated.

Step 7: Add the cooked chicken back to the pan and toss everything together. Cook for an additional minute until everything is heated through.

Simple Stir Fry

METHOD

Step 8: Serve hot over cooked rice or noodles, if desired.

Savory Mushroom Chicken

Prep: 10

Cook: 20

Difficulty: Easy

Serves: 2

Savory Mushroom Chicken

INGREDIENTS

2-3 chicken breasts

0.5 lb white mushrooms, sliced

1/2 cup chicken broth (or white wine, if preferred)

1/4 cup heavy cream

1 shallot, finely chopped

1 tablespoon Dijon mustard

Salt and Pepper

Olive oil or butter for cooking

METHOD

Step 1: In a large skillet, heat olive oil or butter over medium-high heat. Add the chicken breasts seasoned with salt/pepper and sear for about 5-6 minutes on each side, until golden brown and cooked through. Remove from the skillet and set aside.

Step 2: In the same skillet, add a bit more oil or butter if needed. Add the chopped shallot and sauté for 1-2 minutes until translucent. Add the sliced mushrooms and cook for about 5 minutes, until they are tender and have released their moisture.

Step 3: Pour in the chicken broth (or white wine) and bring to a simmer.

Step 4: Stir in the Dijon mustard and heavy cream, mixing well. Allow the sauce to simmer for a few minutes until slightly thickened.

Step 5: Return the chicken to the skillet, coating it with the creamy mushroom sauce. Let it cook for another 2-3 minutes to heat through.

Step 6: Plate the chicken and spoon the creamy mushroom sauce over the top

TIPS & HINTS
- Best served over Asparagus or with Brussel sprouts

Noodles

Creamy Turkey Ditalini

Prep: 10	Difficulty: Easy
Cook: 15	Serves: 4

Creamy Turkey Ditalini

INGREDIENTS

1 lb ground turkey

1/2 red bell pepper (diced)

5 oz fresh spinach

16 oz chicken broth

6 oz white pasta sauce (Store bought or see recipe for white sauce)

1 cup diced tomatoes (canned or fresh)

4 oz dry ditalini pasta

Salt and pepper to taste

1 tablespoon Chili Powder

1 teaspoon Mustard Powder

Olive oil (optional, for cooking)

METHOD

Step 1: In a large skillet or pot, heat a drizzle of olive oil over medium heat. Add the ground turkey and cook until browned, breaking it apart with a spoon. Season with salt, pepper, chili powder and ground mustard.

Step 2: Add the diced red bell pepper to the skillet and sauté for about 3-4 minutes until softened. Stir in the diced tomatoes and cook for another 2 minutes.

Step 3: Pour in the chicken broth and bring the mixture to a boil. Once boiling, add the ditalini pasta. Reduce heat to a simmer and cook according to package instructions, usually around 8-10 minutes, until the pasta is tender.

Step 4: When the pasta is almost done, stir in the spinach and white pasta sauce. Cook for an additional 2-3 minutes until the spinach is wilted and everything is heated through.

Step 5: Taste and adjust the seasoning with more salt and pepper if needed.

Creamy Turkey Ditalini

METHOD

TIPS & HINTS

- Serve hot, garnished with additional spinach or a sprinkle of cheese if desired.

Simple Pad Thai

Prep: 10   Difficulty: Moderate

Cook: 20   Serves: 4

Simple Pad Thai

INGREDIENTS

Ingredients
1 lb Chicken Breats (sliced)

1 tablespoon olive oil or sesame oil

2 eggs, lightly beaten

8 oz rice noodles

1 cup shredded carrots

2 cloves garlic

2 green onions

1 red bell pepper

3 tablespoons soy sauce

1 tablespoon lime juice

1 tablespoon honey

1 tablespoon rice vinegar

1 teaspoon fish sauce

1 teaspoon Sriracha
METHOD

Ingredients
Step 1: Cook rice noodles according to package instructions (typically soak in hot water for 5-7 minutes). Drain and set aside.

Step 2: In a small bowl, whisk together the soy sauce, lime juice, honey, rice vinegar, fish sauce (if using), and Sriracha. Set aside.

Step 3: Heat the olive or sesame oil in a large pan or wok over medium-high heat. Add the sliced chicken and cook for 5-7 minutes, until fully cooked and lightly browned. Remove from the pan and set aside.

Simple Pad Thai

METHOD

Step 4: In the same pan, add the beaten eggs. Scramble them gently, cooking for 1-2 minutes until set. Push the eggs to one side of the pan.

Step 5: Add the garlic, shredded carrots, and bell pepper to the pan. Stir-fry for 2-3 minutes until just softened.

Step 6: Add the cooked chicken, noodles, and sauce to the pan. Toss everything together until well combined and heated through.

Step 7: Garnish with chopped green onions, peanuts, and extra lime wedges. Serve immediately and enjoy!

4-Cheese Brisket Mac and Cheese

Prep: 15

Cook: 35

Difficulty: Easy

Serves: 4-6

4-Cheese Brisket Mac and Cheese

INGREDIENTS

2 cups elbow macaroni

2 cups cooked brisket, shredded (can substitute with pulled pork, chicken, or leave out)

2 tablespoons butter

2 tablespoons all-purpose flour

2 cups whole milk

1 cup shredded sharp cheddar cheese

1/2 cup shredded mozzarella cheese

1/2 cup shredded Gruyère cheese

3/4 cup grated Parmesan cheese

Salt and pepper, to taste

1/2 teaspoon garlic powder

1/2 teaspoon onion powder

1 cup panko breadcrumbs

2 tablespoons melted butter

1 tablespoon fresh parsley

METHOD

Step 1: Preheat your oven to 375°F. Cook the macaroni according to package directions, but slightly undercook it (about 1-2 minutes less than the package suggests). Drain and set aside.

Step 2: In a large saucepan, melt the butter over medium heat. Once melted, whisk in the flour and cook for 1-2 minutes, creating a roux (this will thicken the sauce).

Step 3: Slowly add the milk, whisking constantly to avoid lumps. Cook for 3-5 minutes, allowing the sauce to thicken.

Step 4: Once thickened, lower the heat and add the cheddar, mozzarella, Gruyère, and Parmesan cheeses, stirring until melted and smooth.

4-Cheese Brisket Mac and Cheese

METHOD

Step 5: Stir in the garlic powder, onion powder, and season with salt and pepper to taste.

Step 6: In a large mixing bowl, combine the cooked pasta with the shredded brisket (or other protein). Pour the cheese sauce over the pasta and brisket, and stir to combine, making sure everything is evenly coated. Transfer the mixture into a greased 9x13-inch baking dish.

Step 7: In a small bowl, combine the panko breadcrumbs, melted butter, and Parmesan cheese. Stir until the breadcrumbs are coated. Sprinkle the breadcrumb mixture evenly over the top of the mac and cheese.

Step 8: Place the baking dish in the oven and bake for 20-25 minutes, or until the top is golden brown and the cheese is bubbling. Let the mac and cheese rest for 5 minutes before serving. Garnish with chopped parsley if desired.

TIPS & HINTS

- For extra crunch, you can broil the top for 1-2 minutes at the end (keep an eye on it to avoid burning).

Beef

Quick Beef and Broccoli

Prep: 10

Cook: 15

Marinate: 10-15

Difficulty: Moderate

Serves: 4

Quick Beef and Broccoli

INGREDIENTS

1 lb flank steak or sirloin, thinly sliced against the grain

3 teaspoons sesame oil

4 cups broccoli florets

5 tablespoons soy sauce

3 tablespoons cornstarch

1 teaspoon rice wine or dry sherry

1 tablespoon oyster sauce

1 tablespoon hoisin sauce

1 tablespoon brown sugar

1/2 cup beef broth (or water)

1 teaspoon fresh ginger

2 cloves garlic,

METHOD

Step 1: In a bowl, mix the 2 tablespoons soy sauce, cornstarch, and rice wine (if using). Add the sliced beef and toss to coat. Let it marinate for about 10-15 minutes while you prep the vegetables.

Step 2: In a small bowl, whisk together the 3 tablespoons soy sauce, oyster sauce, hoisin sauce, brown sugar, beef broth, cornstarch, and 1 tablespoon sesame oil. Set this sauce aside.

Step 3: Bring a pot of water to a boil. Add the broccoli florets and cook for 1-2 minutes until bright green and just tender. Drain and set aside.

Step 4: Heat 1 tablespoon sesame oil in a large skillet or wok over medium-high heat. Add the marinated beef in a single layer and sear it for about 2-3 minutes per side until it's browned but not fully cooked through. Remove the beef and set it aside.

Step 5: In the same pan, add the remaining 1 tablespoon sesame oil. Toss in the garlic and ginger and cook for about 30 seconds until fragrant.

Quick Beef and Broccoli

METHOD

Step 6: Return the beef to the pan and add the broccoli. Pour in the sauce and toss everything together. Stir-fry for another 2-3 minutes, allowing the sauce to thicken and coat the beef and broccoli evenly.

Step 7: Serve your beef and broccoli over steamed rice or noodles. Enjoy!

TIPS & HINTS

- Beef options: Flank steak or sirloin are both ideal cuts for this dish because they're tender and easy to slice thinly. You can also use ribeye or skirt steak. Veggie add-ins: Feel free to add other vegetables like bell peppers, onions, or mushrooms for extra flavor and color.

Sauces

White Sauce

Prep: 5

Cook: 5

Difficulty: Easy

White Sauce

INGREDIENTS

2 cups heavy cream

1/2 cup freshly grated Parmesan cheese

Salt to taste

1/4 cup butter

2 tablespoons cornstarch

1/4 cup cold water (for cornstarch slurry)

METHOD

Step 1: In a small bowl, mix the cornstarch with cold water until smooth. Set aside.

Step 2: In a medium saucepan, melt the butter over medium heat. Once the butter is melted, slowly pour in the heavy cream, stirring constantly to combine.

Step 3: Bring the mixture to a gentle simmer. Once it starts to bubble, stir in the cornstarch slurry. Continue to cook, stirring frequently, until the sauce thickens (about 2-3 minutes).

Step 4: Reduce the heat to low, then add the grated Parmesan cheese. Stir until the cheese is fully melted and the sauce is smooth. Season with salt to taste.

Step 5: Use the sauce immediately over pasta, vegetables, or as a base for casseroles. Enjoy!

Peanut Sauce

Prep: 15

Difficulty: Easy

Serves: 4-6

Peanut Sauce

INGREDIENTS

1/2 cup natural, peanut butter

2 tablespoon soy sauce

1 tablespoon rice vinegar

1 tablespoon brown sugar

2 teaspoon chili garlic sauce (adjust to taste)

1 teaspoon lime juice

2 garlic cloves, pressed or grated

1 teaspoon fresh ginger root, grated

2-4 tablespoon warm water (adjust for consistency)

METHOD

Step 1: Combine Ingredients: In a medium bowl, add the peanut butter, soy sauce, rice vinegar, brown sugar, chili garlic sauce, lime juice, grated garlic, and grated ginger.

Step 2: Mix Well: Use a whisk or fork to mix everything together until smooth. Gradually add warm water, 1 tablespoon at a time, mixing until you reach your desired consistency. For a thicker sauce, use less water; for a thinner sauce, add more.

Step 3: Taste the sauce and adjust the flavors if needed. You can add more lime juice for acidity, more chili garlic sauce for heat, or more brown sugar for sweetness.

TIPS & HINTS

- Use this peanut sauce as a dip for veggies, a dressing for salads, or a sauce for noodles or grilled meats. If you have leftovers, store the sauce in an airtight container in the refrigerator for up to a week. Just give it a good stir before using, the oil will separate!

Muffins, Scones and Scrolls

Chocolate Chip Banana Muffins

Prep: 10

Cook: 22

Difficulty: Moderate

Serves: 12

Chocolate Chip Banana Muffins

INGREDIENTS

3 ripe bananas, mashed

1/4 cup Greek yogurt (plain or vanilla)

1/2 cup honey or maple syrup

2 large eggs

2 teaspoons vanilla extract

1 1/2 cups flour

2 teaspoons baking powder

1 teaspoon baking soda

1/2 teaspoon salt

1/2 cup mini chocolate chips

METHOD

Step 1: Preheat your oven to 350°F and line a muffin tin with paper liners or spray with non-stick spray.

Step 2: In a large bowl, combine the mashed bananas, Greek yogurt, honey (or maple syrup), eggs, and vanilla extract. Mix until well combined.

Step 3: In another bowl, whisk together the flour, baking powder, baking soda, and salt.

Step 4: Gradually add the dry ingredients to the wet ingredients, stirring until just combined. Be careful not to overmix. Fold in the mini chocolate chips.

Step 5: Divide the batter evenly among the muffin cups, filling each about 2/3 full.

Step 6: Bake for 20-25 minutes, or until a toothpick inserted in the center comes out clean.

Baking

Simple Pie Crust

Prep: 20

Difficulty: Moderate

Simple Pie Crust

INGREDIENTS

1 1/2 cups all-purpose flour

1/2 cup (1 stick) unsalted butter, chilled and cut into small pieces

1/4 teaspoon salt

2 to 3 tablespoons ice water

1/4 cup granulated sugar (optional for sweet pies)

METHOD

Step 1: In a large bowl, whisk together the flour, sugar (if using), and salt.

Step 2: Add the chilled butter pieces to the flour mixture. Using a pastry cutter, fork, or your fingers, work the butter into the flour until the mixture is in coarse crumbs.

Step 3: Sprinkle 2 tablespoons of ice water over the mixture. Gently stir with a fork.

Step 4: Gather the dough into a ball and flatten it into a disk. Wrap it in plastic wrap and refrigerate for at least 30 minutes.

Step 5: On a lightly floured surface, roll out the dough to fit your pie dish. Transfer it to the dish, trim the edges, and press it into place.

TIPS & HINTS

- If the dough doesn't come together, add a tspn more water, a little at a time, until the dough holds together when pressed.

Simple Pie Crust

INGREDIENTS

1 1/2 cups all-purpose flour

1/2 cup (1 stick) unsalted butter, chilled and cut into small pieces

1/4 teaspoon salt

2 to 3 tablespoons ice water

1/4 cup granulated sugar (optional for sweet pies)

METHOD

Step 1: In a large bowl, whisk together the flour, sugar (if using), and salt.

Step 2: Add the chilled butter pieces to the flour mixture. Using a pastry cutter, fork, or your fingers, work the butter into the flour until the mixture is in coarse crumbs.

Step 3: Sprinkle 2 tablespoons of ice water over the mixture. Gently stir with a fork.

Step 4: Gather the dough into a ball and flatten it into a disk. Wrap it in plastic wrap and refrigerate for at least 30 minutes.

Step 5: On a lightly floured surface, roll out the dough to fit your pie dish. Transfer it to the dish, trim the edges, and press it into place.

TIPS & HINTS

- If the dough doesn't come together, add a tspn more water, a little at a time, until the dough holds together when pressed.

Simple Pie Crust

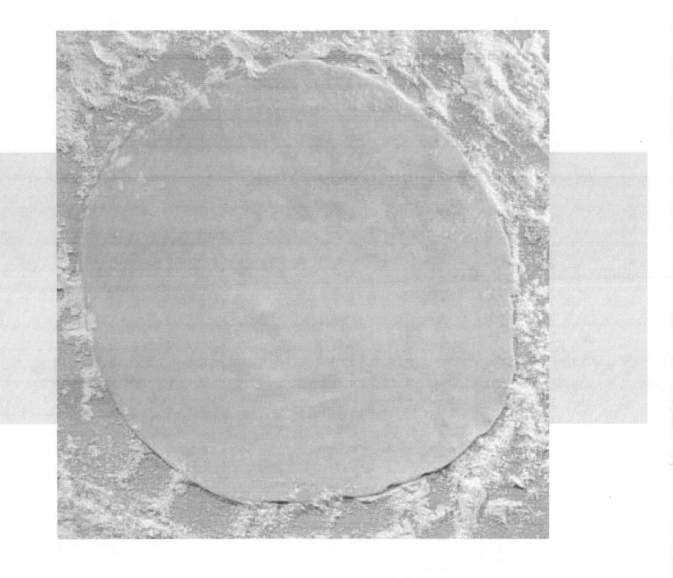

Prep: 20

Difficulty: Moderate

You made it to the end, thank you for being here.
Angelica Kinman

Made in the USA
Monee, IL
23 November 2024

3a7e0307-111a-496f-8039-6c1f56ad28fcR01